I0463267

The Forex Millionaire Maker
By Tony Manso

All Rights Reserved. © 2009-2010 by Tony Manso
Unauthorized copying, reproducing, reselling and distribution prohibited.

Table of Contents

Chapter 1: Who Is This Book For?

I wrote this book specifically for people who are experienced with forex trading, and have won and lost "money" trading. I accent the word "money" because I am not necessarily referring actual money. If you have traded a demo account then you know what I mean. In a demo account you are trading the live markets with simulated money. I have used demo accounts many times in my learning of forex. However, I do not ever recommend to people that they use them. I will get more into that in another chapter. Even so, a demo account is a good way to learn your way around your trading platform, so I cannot discount them completely.

If you are like me, you have had much success trading, and just as much failure or more. You have drained several demo and live accounts after experimenting with an idea and thinking "I've figured it out, now I'm going to make some real money!". You have determined which is your favorite currency pair, and have learned most or all of its secrets. And yet, your live account does not grow. Or even worse, it doubles or triples and then in a single trade is drained completely. Now you have to wait, maybe even for several months, until you have enough money saved up to try again.

If you can identify with the things in the above paragraphs, then this book is written specifically for you.

Chapter 2: About Me

Before I go on babbling about myself, let me get some formalities out of the way. There are some assumptions I am making in this book that might not apply to you. Keep this in mind as you read because although it might seem like am I being literal, I am actually being figurative. Well, here goes...

- As much as possible, I will use the word "leverage". Some people like "gearing", others like "margin", while others prefer something else. Me, I like "leverage".

- As much as possible, I will use "EA" as the abbreviation for "Expert Advisor". An EA is simply a software trading robot that can monitor the markets and place trades for you.

- I speak in "standard lots". In other words, instead of saying "1 mini lot" I will say "0.1 lots".

- I think in USD, even though I generally do not trade USD pairs. More specifically, when I mention the cost of a pip, I generally equate 1 pip to be worth 10 USD at 1 standard lot.

OK, now on to the good stuff. :-)

I am not rich (yet).

As of this writing, I am not some millionaire forex trader who makes all his money off the markets. Today I am a software developer, internet marketer and information technology consultant. Over the years I have learned how to trade as a hobby; stocks, options, and forex. Just in the last few months I realized what I had been missing to become a professional forex trader and worked out a system that I believe will get me my first million dollars in just a few years. This book marks the beginning of that journey. If you have purchased this book then you are invited to learn what I have learned, and also to watch my progress as I practice what I preach. I discovered a way to start with almost nothing, build it up while taking out some for spending, and ending up with a large sum in my account that I can live off for (hopefully) the rest of my life. And I am inviting you to join me for the ride.

I Love Contests!

I have entered many trading contests over the years. Stock, options and forex. I haven't won any (ha ha) but usually I end up in the top 20. One options trading contest I was in had nearly 50000 contestants, and I ended in the top 100. I can't remember exactly what position, though. So naturally, the Automated Trading Competition was something I couldn't resist. Last year (2007) I ended at position 219 out of 603 contestants. I used a martingale EA that I developed but it turned out to be a flop. I had hoped to be able to trade the EA on a live account, but repeated testing proved it could not survive unless I had a win/loss ratio of at least 10:1, which at the time for me was impossible. The funny thing now is that my latest EA, the AME Cross Trader, has a win/loss ratio of about 14:1, so a martingale approach might actually work for it.

To be honest, I never expected the AME Cross Trader to ever make it to first place in the 2008 competition. But I knew from the beginning that it was a way for me to draw attention to this book. Not because I wanted to make a bunch of money selling eBooks, but because I knew that most people who trade forex, even the ones who were competing, had the same problem I did. They know how to place profitable trades. They know how to analyze charts and find good entry points for trades. Some even know how to automate their entry/exit logic with MetaTrader Expert Advisors. And yet, with all this skill and knowledge, their live accounts never grow, or they grow for a while but then they are drained sometime afterwards. I strongly believe I have solved this problem and I will be showing you the one or two things that you are missing, which are keeping you from solving the problem for yourself.

When the AME Cross Trader rose to first place in the first week, I was shocked. The other thing that shocked me was the fact that my equity rose to $81000 in the first week. My expectation for the contest was to (hopefully) make it to the end with a balance of maybe $70 to $90 thousand. I thought it would take the full three months to achieve this result. Never in my wildest imagination would I have thought it would reach my goal in the first week! But then the worst happened (though it wasn't too bad). The trend on GBPJPY reversed sharply for a few days and my EA lost $20000 in a single trade. Right before the contest I had put in some code that says "If you lose $20000 in a single trade, close all trades and never place another trade ever again.". I chose $20000 as an arbitrary number, thinking that in order for this to occur, my balance would already have to be very high, and my trade size would be very large as well. In other words, it would be near the end of the competition and the EA had reached its desired target. This "panic mode" would guarantee that once I reached my target I would stay there, hopefully ending in the top 10 of all contestants. I was right about the balance being high and the trade size being very large, but I was so wrong about it being the end of the competition. So now my EA has stopped in the second week of the competition, and all I can do is sit and watch as the other contestants push me down in the rankings.

Life Before Forex

The Stock Market

I learned all about the stock market years ago and thought it was something I would love to be able to profit from. Originally, I would use the newspaper and look at the stock quotes to find companies that I would like to paper-trade. The only companies that I could see myself consistently making profit from were ones that I couldn't afford to buy. The DOW companies, NASDAQ 100, etc. At the time if I had to pay more than $0.50 per share then I just couldn't afford it. So I never did more than paper-trading when it came to stocks. My success at the time was very limited, and I grew to be somewhat discouraged with the stock market.

Contests! They have contests!

During these times was when I discovered that at any given time there were numerous online trading contests going on. Most of them had cash prizes. I would enter these contests just about every month and do okay but never won anything. It didn't matter. I just love competing when it comes to this kind of stuff.

Options made it possible to "trade stocks"

Later on I learned about options. Now I could spend $1 per share to control a stock that was $20 per share. The risk was fixed. Fixed risk and so much leverage made it very attractive to me, so I opened an account on OptionsXpress.com and started playing with options. But it was nothing more than a hobby. Mostly because I had a family to support and there was no way to raise the kind of money required to make it a career, unless you can profit from the Bimbo Factor, which I'll discuss in a bit. The other thing that made options extremely attractive was the fact that I can buy options on indexes (DIA, SPY, QQQQ), where the strike prices were $1 apart and the Bimbo Factor had almost no effect. There were even options trading competitions, and you already know how much I love contests!

The Dreaded Bimbo Factor

One thing I couldn't stand about the stock market is what I call the Bimbo Factor. Let me explain with a hypothetical situation...

The CEO of a company, whose stock price is $100, has a wife and family. He also has a mistress in every major city that he frequently visits. Everything is going ok until one of his mistresses decides to threaten to expose their relationship to his family. In a panic, he siphons one million dollars from the company's retirement fund to pay off this mistress with a huge diamond ring. Word gets around to the other mistresses and they begin to make the same kinds of threats. In a short while, the company's retirement fund is completely depleted. Two years later the lack of money in the retirement fund is noticed and this triggers an investigation. When the reason for the investigation becomes public knowledge, the stock plummets to $1 per share. Basically, the Bimbo Factor states that one random act from a single "Bimbo" can bring a multi-billion dollar corporation or even an industry to near collapse.

However, not all hope is lost. Given the right Bimbo Factor opportunity, you might be able to buy a $100 stock for $2. And for some reason if the company recovers from the situation, you could potentially have a 5000% return on your investment. Generally speaking, though, that does not happen.

Discovering Forex

One day while watching TV, I saw a commercial for something called 4xMadeEasy, and they were having free seminars in a nearby town. In the commercial they were describing things about forex that were the same things I liked about equity options. What they described implied to me that you can trade on high leverage with no Bimbo Factor. These were things I liked hearing, so I went to the seminar. At the seminar, I liked what I learned about forex, but I didn't like what these people had to offer. They wanted to charge me $3000 for a piece of software that had an indicator that appeared to be triggered by the crossing of two moving averages.

At the end of the seminar, a bunch of people rushed to the rear of the room to order the $3000 software package. I did not. I knew from my stock market experience that these types of "indicators" are available for free for stock and options traders. Why, then, would they not be free for forex? Sure enough, I searched online, and found that almost every forex broker had free tools to do what these guys claimed was their trade secret.

My Forex Education

My first broker

At first I signed up with FXCM. I opened and drained several demo accounts, but eventually got to where I could actively trade and not drain the account. The whole time I was trading demo accounts, I was reading everything I could online about forex trading. I was getting smarter and smarter and it was very exciting. I also noticed that FXCM held monthly trading contests, where cash prizes were given to the highest percentage gainers! However, you had to trade a live account to enter the contest. I wasn't ready to do this. Watching the contests was very inspiring, though. The top contestants were routinely increasing their account by 300% or more, which gave me a small taste of what is possible with forex.

My first live account

After a while practicing with a demo account, I decided it was time to open a live account with $600. The account was drained completely in 4 days. During those 4 days I noticed some very disturbing differences between a demo account and a live account. The first one (and most disturbing) was that it is much more difficult to watch your trades go against you in a live account. The urge to close your trades with a small loss is almost too much to resist. This urge becomes even stronger if you try to hold on to a trade and it continues to move further and further against you.

The second (and most annoying) thing was the fact that the broker would routinely take my stops even if the price was 10 or 15 pips away from my stop price. I still experience that today and have accepted it as a fact of life. However, when you are setting stops at 20-30 pips away, you are just about guaranteeing that your stop will be taken and you will lose money.

Another thing I have noticed recently on other brokers is that they tend to not honor your limit price unless the currency price goes clearly past your limit. I had this happen recently on my live account. On one particular trade, I had a limit that would take me out with over 500 pips profit, and I had a stop loss that locked profits in at about 130 pips. Whichever way the price went I would end in profit. It was a dream trade. However, the price REACHED my limit without triggering, then fell all the way back to the stop price. Because of this, instead of being happy to make any profit, I was furious that my limit did not activate. Instead of being happy that the trade earned me 130 pips, I was upset because it lost me almost 400 pips. I have accepted that to be another fact of life. The brokers are working to keep as much of your money as they can. And if that means giving you 130 pips instead of 500, then it's still an advantage to them.

Draining the next 3 accounts

Over a period of maybe two years I managed to drain another 3 accounts. The last time was just before the 2008 contest (from here on referred to as ATC2008) started. This last time was ok because I had made a withdrawal of my original deposit right before I drained the remainder of the account. So nothing was lost in reality. I will talk about this in detail later but I try to eliminate risk by doubling my account quickly and withdrawing my original deposit. In this case, I doubled my account, took out my deposit, doubled the account again and then got caught by the sunday gap and lost my entire balance. I have seen this same thing happen to several of the contestants in the ATC2008. It is not an isolated incident. But I digress...

Each time I drained an account, I rationalized why it happened or I distorted the truth...

1: Not enough money in the account
I convinced myself that I didn't have enough money in the account. This was true to some degree, because the smallest trade size on FXCM at the time was 0.1 lots. At $1 per pip, you will blow through $600 very quickly. But still, knowing what I know now I could have grown that account 1000% with little difficulty.

2: Ignoring losses and focusing on wins (the gambling mentality)

Why do people love playing roulette? I must admit I love playing myself. It's because it feels wonderful to put down a $10 chip and receive a $350 payout. Notwithstanding you had to lose $700 before you got "lucky". I watch people at the roulette table putting down hundreds of dollars at a time and being handed huge piles of chips when they hit. But when they leave and I ask the dealer how that person really did, the answer is always the same. "He's down by $3000 at least and he'll be here tomorrow to do it again". Don't let the thrill of "winning" in forex do this to you. Forex is your new potential career, and you need to think in terms of "How can I make forex pay my bills and give me a comfortable retirement?"

For the record, when I play roulette, my attitude is "I have $500 for roulette. Let's see how long I can play for before it's all gone". It's not to "win" but for the pleasure of playing the game. I know what I'm willing to pay for that pleasure up front and I stick with it. Sometimes I come home with more than I started, but I don't let that get to my head.

The way people do this with forex is this. They might set their stop loss too close and get stopped out 10 times with a 30 pip loss. However, when the next trade earns them 200 pips they completely disregard the 300 pips that was already lost and only convince themselves that they are good traders. "Look at me I made 200 pips today!". If you are regularly "winning" but your account balance is overall diminishing, then you are NOT a good trader. You are a gambler.

3: Burning through demo accounts like water

The other horrible mistake I made over and over was trading demo accounts while I was raising money for another deposit into my live account. I became so desensitized by demo accounts that I had to teach myself again how to fear losing real money. With a demo account, you open the account, think up a strategy, place some trades, lose all your money then go and open a new account to work on the next strategy. All this does is get you so accustomed to draining accounts that when it happens on a live account, you don't care. You just go back to demo accounts until you have money for another deposit to your live account. Please, please, please do not trade demo accounts unless you are learning a new platform. Nowdays you can open a live account with $250, and place trades of 0.01 lots. This means each pip will earn or lose about $0.10. You can withstand gigantic losses at that price without costing you so much for your "forex education".

Summary

I love forex. I have made every rookie and amateur mistake possible and have (for the most part) learned from my mistakes. I figured out a strategy that I believe will enable me to build up an account balance that can provide a comfortable living for me in the future. And I want to share that strategy with you.

Chapter 3: The Mistakes We Make

When we first learn trading, we tend to make several mistakes that keep us from having any kind of success. In this chapter I will discuss the ones that have affected me the most. Some of these I still struggle with. However, most of the ones I struggle with are ones that an EA can keep me from experiencing.

Mistake #1: Too much leverage

As of this writing, some brokers such as FxPro will let you trade 1 full lot for every $200 in your account. This is 1:500 leverage! As exciting as it sounds, it is the easiest way to drain your account. For example, suppose I have $10000 in my account at 1:500 leverage. I could place a trade of 25 lots and only tie up half of my available equity. At this size, each pip would be worth $250. If you bought EUR/USD with a 3 pip spread, it would cost you $750 just to place the trade. Think of it this way, with $5000 tied up in the trade and $5000 free equity, each pip represents FIVE PERCENT of your available equity! That means you would get a margin call after losing just 20 pips!

I have a rule about leverage. I never trade more than 1:10 leverage. That means $10000 cash in the account for each 1 lot I trade. That being the case, starting with $500 means you can trade 0.05 lots, which amounts to about $0.50 per pip. That only leaves room for about a 500 pip loss. That means high risk at first, but if you can think of it as a $500 total risk, then it won't be so scary. I'll talk more about this later.

Mistake #2: Getting in NOW. Not waiting

There are two problems that most people have when it comes to patience as it pertains to trading. Especially those who trade the 4-hour or daily charts.

Problem 1: Not waiting to enter

It could take weeks for a strong entry signal to occur, and we don't want to wait that long. We don't want to wait at all! We want to get in right now. So we guess what the next signal is going to be and trade in such a way that when that signal comes, we are already in position to take advantage of the situation. Let me tell you right now THIS DOESN'T WORK.

Problem 2: Not waiting to exit

Once a trade is placed, watching the price fluctuate up and down 20, 30, 50 pips will drive you to drink. Heavily. If you don't know your exit when you place a trade then it might do you some good to step away for at least an hour before making any decisions. My EA, the AME Cross Trader, places a trade then waits for one complete bar to pass before deciding if it's time to set take-profit or begin a trailing stop. Also, when you place a trade, there's only a 50% chance that the trade will move in your favor right from the beginning. It's easy to panic and think you were wrong when the trade immediately goes against you. But if you determined the trend correctly, the trade should come back in your favor. Of course you will endure some drawdown while the trade is open, but if your account can handle the drawdown you should be ok.

Someone once said "Good things come to those who wait". In forex this is true wisdom. Being impulsive will cost you dearly. Knowing when to wait and when to "jump ship" will save you a lot of grief (and money) in the long run.

Mistake #3: Tight fixed stops

When I first started trading, I would place an order with a 20 or 30 pip stop loss. In almost every case, my stop would be taken and the price would immediately go in my favor and take off in my desired direction. Without me. I would get frustrated, place a new market order with a 30 pip stop loss and watch it happen again and again. Instead of gaining 100 pips or more in a single trade, I would lose 100 pips or more in multiple attempts to catch a move in my chosen direction. Assuming you have calculated the trend correctly, you need to be willing to endure some drawdown before the price moves in your favor. This is especially true if you are trading 1-hour charts or higher. If you set your stop loss at the time of placing your order, then there is a great chance that you will be taken out of the trade with a loss, even if the price moves in the direction you were aiming for.

Mistake #4: Not knowing your exit

Before I get into this, I have to admit that this is a very tricky and elusive thing that depends much on your attitude towards winning. Let me tell you a story that demonstrates my point...

> *A man and his new bride were celebrating their honeymoon at a casino. After they had consummated their marriage, the bride fell asleep and the husband was wide awake, so he went downstairs to the casino with $2 that was left over from gambling.*

He went to the roulette table and placed the $2 on a single number and won, leaving him with $70. He placed the $70 on a new number and won again, leaving him with $1750. This amazing luck continued over and over with black-jack, poker, and other games until he was in possession of over $30000. Finally, he bet all his money on roulette and lost it all in a single bet.

The man went back upstairs to his hotel room and when he shut the door, his wife woke up. When she asked where he had been, he told her he couldn't sleep so he went downstairs to gamble. When she asked how he did, he said "I lost $2".

In this same manner, I can place a trade, risking a fixed amount of money. If I lose then I have lost the amount I was willing to lose and nothing more. If I am ahead by, say, 100 pips, I can begin a 70 pip trailing stop. This way I have locked in at least 30 pips profit. This becomes my expectation. Nothing more. If the price continues to move in my favor then I might end with more than 30 pips profit and have a big smile on my face. But if the price immediately goes against me and stops me out, I can't complain about the 70 pips I just gave up. I knew my exit and that's exactly what I got.

My Expert Advisor (The AME Cross Trader) does something unusual in terms of locking in profit, which I will explain briefly here. Suppose it places a buy order at the open of a new bar. The assumption is that we are in an uptrend. At the open of the next bar, the AME Cross Trader looks to see if the high of the bar that just completed is at least a certain number of pips above my opening price. If this is the case then I set that high as my limit. The reason is that if we are indeed in an uptrend, unless something unusual happens, the price will reach this level again. I have found this to be true as much as 14 out of 15 times in some currency pairs. By doing this I can capture profits earlier than if I use a trailing stop, then be ready to trade again immediately.

To summarize, when I say "know your exit" I don't necessarily mean to know before you place your trade. The AME Cross Trader, for example, waits for at least one full bar to complete before deciding how much profit can be hoped for. Sometimes it takes more than a single bar and tries to set a trailing stop to lock in profit while trying to decide where the ideal exit is. The point I am making is that you should not wait too long after a trade is placed to decide to take profits. Trailing stops are nice but limit orders sure feel better when they are hit. There is a psychological reason for this. Stop loss, even when profit is locked, is hit when the trade is going against you. Limits are hit when the trade is going in your favor. The latter just **feels** better than the former. :-)

Mistake #5: Trusting an EA for the long term

This is another touchy subject. I do believe that an EA can be used for long term growth and cash flow. However, I am not in a position to use one of those. The reason I say this is because at this time I only have a small amount of money to trade with, and this book is about the process of turning $500 into $1000000. A "long term" EA cannot do this with $500. A long term EA will work wonderfully with $50000 or $100000 and create a nice cash flow that we might be able to live on. Unfortunately, the people I wrote this book for do not have $50000 laying around that they can deposit into their forex accounts. We need to rely on a different method that will enable us to build up to, say, $50000, $100000 or even $1000000 so that we can then apply a stable, low-risk EA that will pay our bills for the rest of our lives.

Mistake #6: Using a demo account to simulate real trading

This is where most of my opposition comes from. Everyone says you should use a demo account before you start trading live. I say "yes" but not for the sake of "pretending" to trade a live account. There are some *critical* elements missing from demo trading that cannot be simulated. We'll get to that in a bit. Here's what you *should* use a demo account for...

- **Forward testing your EA**: Forward testing of your EA should be done for a time on a demo account, to make sure that you have all your EA parameters set correctly, and to make sure the EA behaves the way you expect it to, especially if you are testing out a new broker. Make sure that the demo account is with the same broker that you have your live account with. This way there will be (almost) no surprises when you switch from demo to live trading.

- **Mastery of manual trading**: There's going to be times when you are trading manually, even if it is only to intervene with a decision that your EA makes. Since this is the case, you need to be good at placing, modifying and closing orders. So good that you can do it in your sleep. A live account is no place for you to place an order of 5 lots when you intended to place a 0.5 lot order, or to place a buy order when you intended on placing a sell order. These types of "rookie" mistakes can be easily overcome on a demo account.

Also, there are two really important things that absolutely cannot be simulated on a demo account. I know many people who disagree with this but this has been my personal experience. I don't think yours will vary :-)

- **Draining and replenishing your account**: As I mentioned in a previous chapter, I got so accustomed to draining demo accounts and opening new ones, that it affected my live trading drastically. If you drain a demo account, you can simply open a new one with however much money you desire. If you drain a live account, you have to spend weeks or even months saving up enough money to make another deposit into the account so you can trade again. Also, your confidence in trading is diminished, your likelihood to panic when a trade goes against you increases, and your overall judgement is impaired. If you use a live account with tiny trade sizes (0.01 lots for example) then you can experience all of the emotions that go with winning and losing real money, and learn gradually and inexpensively to deal with them until you can overcome them. People will argue "why risk real money to learn a strategy?", but I say you're risking even more "real" money by doing it with a demo account.

- **Watching the pips come and go**: With a demo account you can place an order of 5 lots and watch your pips come and go with almost no emotion. But on a live account, an order of 0.1 lots means watching your hard earned dollars come and go over and over, taking you on an emotional roller coaster ride that might eventually cause you to jump off the ride before it is safe to do so. The roller coaster is a good analogy because if you try to jump off anytime before the ride is over, you will get hurt. Badly. But if you just wait until the ride is over then no harm will come to you. Such can easily be the case with forex trading.

Mistake #7: Back testing and optimizing on a demo account

Never, ever, ever use a demo account for back testing or optimizing an EA. Always use a live account. Always use THE live account that you will be running your EA on. Always make sure you are *logged into* the live account before you run a back test or optimization. The reason for this is that the back tester and optimizer both appear to use the MarketInfo() data from the last account you were logged into. Many brokers do not have identical MarketInfo() values between their live and demo accounts. If you don't know what that means then just trust me on this one. It might not seem like much but in back test, a slight difference in pip size, margin level, stopout level, etc. could make the difference between quadrupling your live account or draining it. Or it could mean the difference between all of your orders working on demo but failing to execute on live.

Mistake #8: Never taking profits

Taking profits to me is more than just closing a profitable order. This is probably the most likely reason you, or the majority of traders cannot grow their accounts.

A new concept; Withdrawals

When trading forex, there is misconception about the term "withdrawal". People are convinced that if they take out some of their money, their EA or their trading style will be hindered because they cannot take advantage of larger trade sizes. From my perspective, withdrawing money from your account is something that will happen with or without you. It is a race between you and your broker to see who can "withdraw" the money from your account first.

Here is an example: You are a trend follower and you increase your account by 200% over a month's time. Then the trend changes to work against you. One of two things WILL happen. The reversal will "withdraw" most or all of your money and give it to the broker, or YOU will "withdraw" your money and keep it for yourself.

If you can repeatedly withdraw money, while keeping enough in the account to continue trading, then you are already well on your way towards a career in forex trading. If you take money out of your account, you cannot lose that money by trading. This is what the brokers fail to tell you when they lure you in to open accounts with them. It is not in their best interest for you to withdraw money. It is in their best interest for THEM to withdraw your money. And they work hard to do this.

Summary

Once you can keep from making these mistakes, then you will have taken your forex trading to the next level.

Chapter 4: Learning To Trade (again)

As I mentioned at the beginning of this book, if you are reading this then you probably already know how to trade. You have opened and traded a live account, and can actively trade the account without draining it. Even if you have drained accounts in the past, at least by now you should know how NOT to drain your account. Also, you need to know the difference between trading by a system and trading by emotions.

You already know how to trade

At this point you know all about trading and can keep from draining your live account. However, the problem seems to be that you can't grow the account without eventually losing most or all of your gains. There is a reason for this and I will discuss it in the section that teaches how I myself trade.

Developing your "system"

Once you can trade without emotion, it's time to look at developing a method whereby you will trade from here until some monetary goal has been met. This system will be one that drastically increases the chances of your account growing steadily.

Select a currency pair and master it

Everyone has different taste when it comes to trading styles. Certain currency pairs tend to work better with certain trading styles, and each pair has its own level of risk associated with it. For example, my favorite pair is GBPJPY, but it is probably the one that carries the most risk. The reason is the speed at which it violently fluctuates. It is not uncommon for a single bar on the 4-hour chart to have a range of 300 pips! But GBPJPY is also very trendy on the 4-hour and daily charts, so if you can endure the drawdown, you can capture a tremendous amount of pips in a short time.

The USD pairs such as GBPUSD and EURUSD tend to be trendy as well. However, these are extremely sensitive to news announcements. These announcements tend to cause the price to spike wildly in one direction or the other, regardless of trend direction. On these pairs it is not uncommon to see a single bar on the chart that has 5 times the trading range of all the bars surrounding it. These spikes have a tendency to trigger your stops with a loss, even if your trade was very much in profit before the spike.

Then there are currency pairs like EURGBP, which seem like very slow moving, calm and easy to trade. However, pips on EURGBP are very expensive compared to other pairs! You need to adjust your trade size accordingly if you want to trade EURGBP or it might trick you into a margin call.

The point I am trying to make is that you need to find a pair that works with your risk level, and learn its behavior inside and out. Find as much information as you can on the internet, from books or from mentors to see if anyone has come up with a reliable way to determine entry and exit for your favorite pair. Then you can adapt these methods and come up with your own variations. But the important thing is you need to be able to look at a chart and within 5 seconds KNOW if it's a good time to place a trade or if you need to stay out of the market. Ok maybe a little time to plot your favorite indicators on the chart, but no more than that! :-)

Determine a pattern for entry and exit

Once you become familiar with the currency pair or pairs that you will be trading, you will need to look for reoccurring patterns that happen before or around the time of each entry. For example, when I use the two moving averages, I look for the last completed bar to be completely outside of both moving averages. I also look for the shorter moving average to be in between the bar and the longer moving average. This is my entry signal. However, at this point it is too late to turn on my EA, so I need to find something that happens **before** this signal so that I can turn on my EA and it can wait for the signal to place the trade. Usually this signal is preceded by a bar that has one of the moving averages going through it. When I see this condition on the chart, that is my cue to turn on the EA so that it can do its thing when the entry signals start coming. The screen shot below shows this graphically.

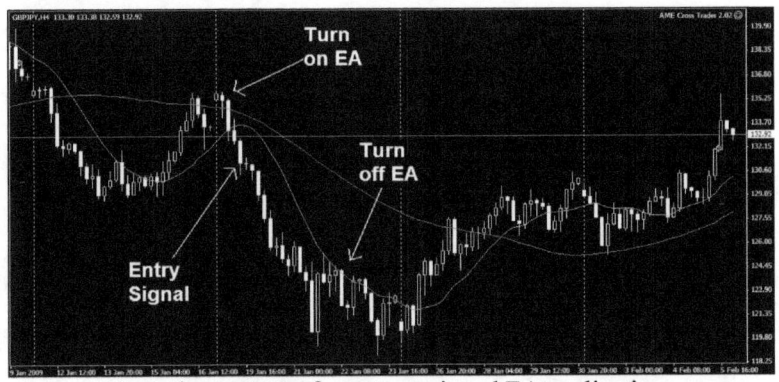

Locating patterns for entry, exit and EA application

Use your system ONLY when it works.

As you can see in the graphic above, there is a place where I turn on my EA and a place where I am most likely to turn it off. I use the EA to implement **some** of my strategy for me, but ultimately I decide when it runs and when it does not. Likewise, my system only works when the charts look a certain way. When the charts don't look right then I don't trade. Period.

Decide when to take profits and stick with it

My EA, the AME Cross Trader, works wonderfully during a trendy market. It uses the profits earned in previous trades to multiply profits in future trades. It can quadruple your account in as little as a few weeks. If you followed the Automated Trading Championship in 2008, you saw firsthand how the EA generated 700% profits in about 8 days! But eventually (without panic mode) it will place one or two trades in a row that will completely drain your account.

So you are probably wondering "Why use such a risky EA?", and the answer is simple. It does ONE thing very well. Earn money. But only when conditions are right. Remember when I said "Use your system only when it works"? I use my EA to reach a specific goal, either double or triple my account. Then I close all trades, turn off the EA, withdraw money from the account, and WAIT until I have the money in my hands before turning the EA on again. I might even wait until the price touches one of the moving averages again.

The point I am trying to make here is you have to know, before you start trading, exactly when you are going to take money out of the account. Remember when I said that your money will be withdrawn one way or another? It will go either into your hands or into your broker's. Decide on your target for withdrawal **before** your broker does it for you.

Decide how big to grow your account

Remember, you will be opening your account with $500 or $1000. This is by no means enough to earn even a modest living by trading. So here is an example of how to calculate how large your account should be in order to sustain your current (or desired) lifestyle.

Suppose I need $4000 per month to survive:

First I need to determine what percentage gains I can safely produce each month. For this example, let's assume that I can easily generate at least 5% gains monthly. To calculate my account size, I use this simple formula...

- *(2m / g) = b* where m is the desired **m**onthly income, g is the percentage **g**ains that you can consistently earn, and b is the minimum **b**alance you need to keep in the account in order to maintain the desired income level.

With this amount in the account, you should be able to earn double your monthly requirement each month. This allows you to spend a month's worth of income and still have enough saved for another month in case the next month is a losing month, or does not completely reach your goal.

Once you know these numbers, you can simply use my system to grow your account to that size, then trade very conservatively and be able to withdraw enough money each month to maintain a comfortable lifestyle.

In our example, I need to earn $4000 each month to live on. The calculation is (2 * 4000 / 0.05) = 160000. In order to be able to withdraw $4000 per month from the account, I have to build my account up to at least $160000 and earn 2.5% per month. However, since my goal is 5% I will hopefully be earning double what is required and saving any excess to use when my trading is not going so well.

Turn your strategy into a process

Once you have a strategy worked out, you need to think of it as a process that you must (generally) follow to the letter. Let me give you an example based on my current "process"...

1. Wait for price to touch one of the moving averages.

2. Turn on the EA.

3. EA waits for entry signal and starts placing trades.

4. Wait for account to triple.

5. Turn off EA and close all trades.

6. Initiate a withdrawal from the broker for a portion of my profits.

7. Wait until money is removed from the account

8. Repeat steps 1 through 7

Of course, tripling my account will not happen every time, and I need to have a strategy for when things go wrong. But the point is you have to define the steps of your process and follow them blindly. At least until the process stops working.

Automate what you can

Like I mentioned earlier, I use my EA to automate the actual trading and the money management portions of my strategy. This frees me up to do other things (like have a life) and keeps me from having to calculate trade sizes every time I place a trade, and more importantly it keeps me from experiencing a lot of the emotions that tend to go along with managing open trades. I do not have to figure out trade size, stop-loss, take-profit or anything else. I only need to know when conditions are right for trading and what is my profit target for making a withdrawal. And most importantly, I need to know **the process**, but I already talked about that. :-)

Know your EA inside and out

Seriously, you need to treat your EA as if it is your clone that you are training to be exactly like you. That means you know exactly what it will do and when. You should be able to look at your chart that has the EA running on it and say something like "In 1 hour it will move stop to 1.9876 and set limit at 1.9700", or "At 16:00 it will place a buy-market order for 1.6 standard lots". Even if you are not the author of the EA, you need to be extremely confident in your ability to predict exactly what it will do at any given time. Without this knowledge, you will not have any idea when it should be turned off.

Summary

Find **your** process and stick with it until it no longer works for you, or until you die. Whichever comes first. If you can streamline or automate parts of your process over time, then by all means do so.

Chapter 5: Using an Expert Advisor

An Expert Advisor (EA) is not necessary for trading, but it can have valuable benefits if you use one. For example, once the EA is running, you are free to do other things with your time. You do not have to experience the emotional roller coaster that goes along with trading in general. You can be placing trades while you sleep. But it is important that you not rely on your EA for anything more than automating some or all of your trading process. Of course there are exceptions to this rule, such as an advanced neural net EA, which learns and adapts to changing market conditions. But for the sake of this book I will assume that your EA is a lot "dumber" than that. :-)

It is NOT the Expert, YOU are

Do I really need to speak more on this? The bottom line is if you do not know how your EA operates then you are at its mercy. That is not a position I want to be in, and neither should you.

It IS the Advisor

I emphasize this here because some people really believe that an EA cannot make a stupid decision. They think that since the decision was made by an EA, it must be the best possible decision. I cannot tell you how many times I have looked at my chart and said "Are you crazy?", then closed whatever trade was just placed by an EA. There have also been times where I look at the chart and see that the EA is *about* to place a stupid trade. So I simply turn it off and wait for the next *intelligent* time to turn it on.

It's a productivity tool

Think of your EA as a tool to enhance your own productivity. You can do everything it does by yourself without help, but there's no need to because you have this "tool" that can do it for you. Here is an analogy to explain it another way...

The electric pencil sharpener analogy

Think about an electric pencil sharpener. It does not know when a pencil needs sharpening. It does not know when it is done sharpening your pencil. If you do not take the pencil out, the sharpener will reduce it down to almost nothing. All it knows is how to sharpen the pencil you put in it. And it can do that as good as or better, and much faster than you can. Think of your Expert Advisor in the same way. You tell it what currency pair to trade, when to trade and when to stop trading.

It reduces your time and effort

Using an EA is probably the easiest and best way to reduce the time and effort required for you to be trading forex. If at all possible, you should perfect your system using manual trading only. Then once you have a high level of confidence in your system, then you can decide if parts of it can be automated. There are people all over the world who love writing Metatrader 4 code, who might be able to automate parts of your strategy. At least your entry/exit and money management strategies can be easily automated. Just this one thing will dramatically free up your time and energy. Not only that, but your EA will be able to place trades 24 hours per day, even while you sleep. But remember, it is entirely up to you to decide when to turn your EA on and off.

Summary

Using an Expert Advisor (EA) is highly recommended for the trading and money management portions of your strategy. This is especially true if you have worked these things out for yourself manually and have then proceeded to automate them. Either way, with an EA you can avoid the emotional roller coaster that generally comes with trading, and that in itself is reason enough to use one. :-)

Chapter 6: How I Trade

This section describes how I personally trade as of this writing. As I examine charts and try to predict what will happen with the currency pairs, I notice patterns. These patterns are the things that help me decide things like when to open and/or close a trade, how large a trade to place, etc. People have been doing this for centuries, so I am not saying that any of this is new. Sometimes, though, re-inventing something is a way for you to gain a powerful testimony of it.

In 2008, I wrote my latest EA, the AME Cross Trader. During certain times it would produce unbelievable gains for a very short time, then almost immediately drain the entire account or get a margin call in a single trade. For the most part, it still does this. I tried making it more reliable, but the more reliable I made it, the less overall gains it produced. I needed to find a good balance but had no luck in doing so. Finally I realized I had been looking at it all wrong. I had been looking to create a "Holy Grail", just like everyone else. No one has ever been able to do this. Why should I suddenly be the first?

Instead, I realized that I had developed a powerful "productivity tool" that took what I could already do and multiply my efforts many times over, and could instantly handle the money management with a precision that only a computer could. So instead of trying to make it work all the time, which I was not having any luck doing, I realized that this "tool" should only be used when "needed", like a pencil sharpener for example. If I use a pencil sharpener on a pencil that's already sharp, all that will be accomplished is to reduce the size of my pencil. Likewise, if I do not apply my EA at the correct times, it will reduce my account to nothing. Simply put, I was spending my energy on perfecting a tool that was already perfect for what it was designed for. What I really needed was to perfect the application of the tool. This is different from how traders generally tend to think. Let me see if I can apply the pencil sharpener analogy more directly to trading...

- The pencil represents your account.

- The lead in the pencil represents your profits.

- The wood of the pencil represents the market.

- The sharpener represents your EA or trading style.

- Writing with the pencil represents the use of your profits.

Essentially, when you use a pencil, you are really only concerned with the lead that's inside the pencil, since that is what actually puts the mark on the paper. It is the part that you are actually **doing** something with. This is not unlike the profits from your trading. The wood of the pencil is actually an obstacle that tends to keep the pencil from writing unless you shave away parts of the wood to expose the lead. The wood is the part you must **overcome** to be able to use the lead. This is not unlike the market or your broker. As you use the pencil, the lead diminishes, just like your profits (generally speaking). At some point you will need to shave away more wood to reveal more lead. Likewise, you need to trade the market to produce more profits. To shave the wood from the pencil, you can either spend 5 *minutes* shaving off pieces of wood with a knife, razor blade, teeth, etc. Or you can spend 5 *seconds* with an electric sharpener and get a much better result.

Now comes the interesting part. If you want to make the best use of that pencil, you need to know exactly when to take it out of the electric sharpener. If you do not take it out at all, you will have no pencil left to write with. The longer you wait to take it out, the more lead you are "giving away" to the pencil sharpener. Is this starting to sound like trading? When you use the electric sharpener, you have a good idea what your goal is; a nice sharp, exposed lead tip. Once that goal is reached, that sharpener gets left alone until its "services" are needed again, and the pencil gets **used**. Your goal with trading should be to reach a profit target, then **do something** with (at least some of) those profits.

Okay, so on to my techniques.

Spotting the trend

I like to use two moving averages when I trade. One short and one a little longer. Sometimes I like to use the 200SMA to decide which direction to trade. Generally speaking, I will only use the 4-hour and daily charts to figure out trend. In the chart below, you will notice 3 moving averages. They are the 6 (orange), 12 (red) and 200 (blue). The position of the last completed bar, relative to the MA200 determines which direction to trade. If the bar is above the MA200 then I will only place buy orders. If the bar is below then I will place sell orders. In cases where I do not use the MA200, trade direction is determined by the position of the last completed bar relative to the MA6 and MA12. If the bar is above both moving averages, then I only place buy orders. If it is below both then I place only sell orders. If it is touching either or in between them, I do nothing.

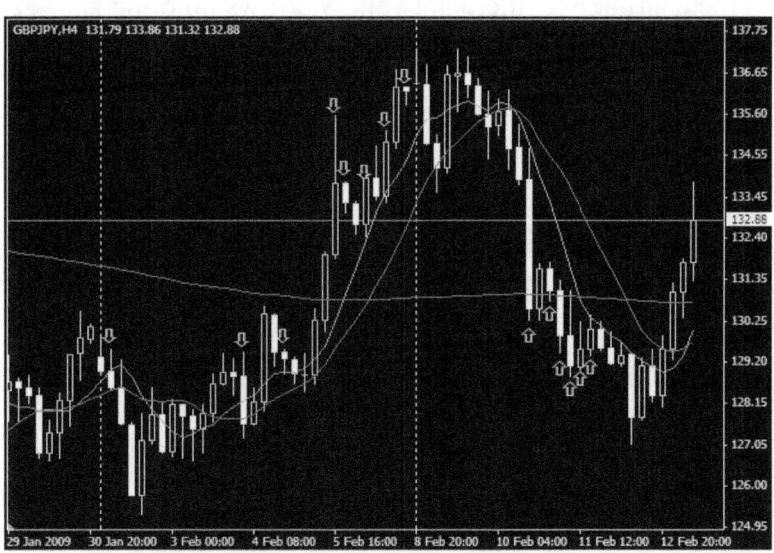

Chart showing moving averages and entry points

Calculating entry and exit

In order to calculate entry, I simply check the last completed bar's position relative to the two moving averages. Here is the basic idea...

- Place a buy order at the formation of a new bar when the last completed bar is not touching either of the moving averages (6 or 12 in the above chart), is above both, and also the shorter moving average is in between the bar and the longer moving average.

- Place a sell order at the formation of a new bar when the last completed bar is not touching either of the moving averages, is below both and the shorter moving average is in between the bar and the longer moving average.

In the chart above, there are yellow arrows pointing at some of the bars. These arrows represent entry signals. An arrow pointing down to the top of a bar represents a buy signal. An arrow pointing up to the bottom of a bar represents a sell signal.

As far as exit signal goes, I generally wait for at least the first bar of the open trade to complete, then determine my exit based on the price action.

Also, I tend to use the 6 and 12 moving averages more often than not, because when I optimize the short and long term moving averages on my EA, I end up with a lot of winning combinations that have a short term moving average of either 6 or 12.

Setting take-profit and stop loss

Before the days of the AME Cross Trader, I was studying charts and noticed something interesting. The high and low of a completed bar is almost never the opening or closing price of that same bar. This means that, for example, during an uptrend you can place a buy order at the open of a new bar and can expect with a high degree of probability that the price will eventually move up to the high of the previous bar. The opposite is true for a downtrend. It doesn't even matter if a bar closes in the trend direction. Before I realized this, I was placing orders immediately after a crossing of the moving averages and staying in the trade until I got a signal for placing a trade in the opposite direction. This works great during long trends, but let me show you how the new way can work even better for you.

Chart showing entry, exit, stop-loss and take-profit.

Look at the chart above. Each blue arrow represents an entry point. Each red arrow represents an exit point. Why didn't I just buy at the first blue arrow and close at the fifth red arrow? One reason only... Each trade can be bigger in size than the winnng trade before it, based on the fact that your account is now bigger. If I had placed a single order and waited for exit, I might have made a nice profit, but not as much as if I closed each trade with a profit and used that profit to apply toward the next trade size.

Also notice the little red lines on the chart above. Those are the stop-loss and take-profit for each trade. The initial stop-loss is set far away from the price. The take-profit is actually set at the open of the next bar after the trade is placed. Take-profit is always (when possible) at the high of the bar that the trade was opened on, which cannot be determined until that bar is complete. Stop-loss is always based on the lowest price reached in the previous 6 bars (in the above example). This is true for buy orders. The opposite is true for sell orders.

Trailing stop

As mentioned before, the initial stop-loss is the high or low of some previous number of bars. In the above example, it is 6 bars. However, I also use a trailing stop technique to lock in profits while waiting for the price to reach the take-profit level. Here is how it works.

Suppose I place a buy order at the open of a bar. At the next bar I set take-profit, but the price does not reach that take-profit level for at least several more bars. While I am waiting, I am also looking for opportunities to move my stop-loss. As soon as a completed bar has a low that is above my open price, I move my stop-loss to the low of that bar. At this point I cannot lose money on this trade (not taking into account a negative swap). I then continue to move my stop-loss at each new bar, provided the low of the newly completed bar is higher than my current stop-loss level.

Millionaire in 11 withdrawals

Remember the pencil and the sharpener? You only sharpen it to use it. Likewise, if you don't **use** the money that you've gained then your broker will find a way to take it away from you. So here's what I came up with.

Suppose I deposit $500 into my account and trade the account until I have three times my original deposit ($1500). Believe me this is not as hard as it sounds and does not have to take a long time either. Once I triple my account, I can take out my original deposit and I have double my original deposit remaining in the account. I am now trading with free money. No more risk. Now suppose I triple my account again ($3000) and withdraw a third ($1000). Then triple again ($6000) and withdraw a third ($2000), and on and on until I finally withdraw $512000. Believe it or not, that is only the 11th withdrawal! Not only that, but by the time you reach that $512000 withdrawal, you will have *already withdrawn* at least $511500! And even better is this... At this point you will have *withdrawn* over $1000000, AND still have another $1000000 in your account!

Of course this is not going to be easy. But let me tell you this. Using the technique I mentioned in this chapter, there is no reason why you couldn't triple your account in 12 weeks or less. That means one withdrawal every 3 months. Four withdrawals per year for three years and you are a millionaire. It doesn't sound so impossible when you look at it that way, does it? And what happens if you make four withdrawals then drain the remainder of your account? You have still turned $500 into $7500! Can you really complain about that? Also do you think you can spare $500 of that and start over again?

But wait, there more! (I love saying that!) I believe that by the time you have made your third withdrawal, you will become an expert at tripling your account, thus making it somewhat easier to do it the next few times. But it's not likely that you'll ever have to triple your account 11 times. Here's why...

The end goal: Career trader and investor

Go back to the section in this book called "Decide how big to grow your account" and you will quickly see that you do not need to grow your account to $1000000. I just use that amount to show that it could happen in three years if you really want it to. But in reality, you may only need to achieve seven withdrawals or less to reach your goal.

Summary

Remember, you only need to grow your account to an amount that will enable you to maintain a comfortable lifestyle by withdrawing enough from your account to live on for a month at a time. I will try to grow my account to $1000000 just for the sake of example. My hope for you is that you will use this information to enable yourself to retire from your day job and become a professional trader, placing trades via your laptop while on your Caribbean cruise. :-)

Also, if just one of my readers uses my strategy to become a millionaire, I will truly be able to call myself "The Forex Millionaire Maker". So what are you waiting for? Go and make money for yourself and a name for me!

I hope this book has inspired you to make something happen with your forex trading. At the least, I hope this has helped you to understand why your account has not been growing. Like I said before, you already had everything you needed to reach your financial goals. You just needed to see things from a different point of view; An investor's point of view, not your broker's point of view.

Chapter 7: For More Information

In support of the readers of this book and the community of traders I am hoping to build, I am keeping a blog for things pertaining to my trading.

http://www.Millionaire-Maker.org/blog

From the blog you will be able to see what I'm currently doing in the forex space, and there is a mailing list signup form that you can fill out to be notified of updates to my blog, products, software and receive cool free stuff.

www.ingramcontent.com/pod-product-compliance
Lightning Source LLC
Chambersburg PA
CBHW051249170526
45165CB00004B/1629